WALTON WELL

CULTURE ART POETRY FICTION SOCIAL JUSTICE

PRESS

HERE IN MY BODY
IT FEELS CROWDED

ALSO BY KAREN KEVORKIAN

White Stucco Black Wing
Lizard Dream
Quivira

HERE IN MY BODY
IT FEELS CROWDED

Karen Kevorkian

WALTON WELL PRESS
Los Angeles   Oxford

Cover art copyright © 1982 Judy Dater, *Self-portrait with Stone*, gelatin silver print, 16 x 20 in.
Design & Typesetting: ash good

Theresia de Vroom
Published by Walton Well Press
Los Angeles | Oxford

Paperback ISBN: 978-1-964295-09-1

WALTONWELLPRESS.COM

Contents

a new shadow behind the usual shadow

—Tomas Tranströmer

The cloud isn't always
a faithful dog.

—Yannis Ritsos

Stunned Awake

Not having the book not remembering what it said

stunned awake into sheets like tissue wrapping of the old dress

dank from years' saving

dusty gritty cement floor little windowless room who knew

what children could get up to

crack of sunlight outside stairs leading down to it

push open the door whatever took place still lingering

don't you feel this way about certain spaces

you would not know what to say to who you once were

a life that could have resembled anyone's

where your body led you too young to have imagined anything

rearing like a car alarm a sweeping fire

over dry grass where you live now

Geometry

Small motors for taming grass moan the day not yet so hot, in the *Times* columns of the
dead are short ones

dried fronds droop at the tops of palms, brown petticoats to fall on walkers when
Santa Anas send husks flying

the dream with a bride upended long white veil trailing, a dance review where *Apollo and
muses create expertly crafted geometry with their bodies*

the friend not seen for a long time, a tanned and lipsticked face

amiably removing a sleek wig from her bald skull, *it makes me so hot* the mouth's little sounds
like water stumbling

past windows green and black snakelike leaves, brushstrokes from a phallic era of painting

seismic rustle of crow feathers, gray ficus trunks' easy to carve into, names overlay names

coiled roots slashed to fit corridors between sidewalks and curbs

here in my body it feels crowded, a recycle truck's slithering cataracts of glass

Starting With a Casual Question

Lying side by side on a July night it started with a casual question asked politely.

He had an ipad ready for the evening's word game. Look he said.

Only 1 day I am not certified a genius. Did you get work done today.

She said she was in that empty place of work completed could not face one more beginning

thought she tried too hard spoke of missteps sidesteps and distractions her voice in neutral gear.

She wanted to be clear she was not asking

to command in other ways. She droned on they lay still

two figures on a tomb. Not the sly Etruscans pleasure implied in posed proximity

or supine Gothic bodies' testament to duty and position. Naked unsunned plump selves

heat-bloomed beneath the soothing diligence of a ceiling fan. He said he read her

she said no he didn't. He said he did she said nothing she did not know whether

or how much she cared. Their life together was one of skin. In recent dreams

he said he held the body of his dead friend. She lay an arm across him.

What did you feel when you woke up. She turned to the side to see his face

he did not wear a mask of knowing. She made a basket of her arms

the shift of lamplight on the hardwood floor of ill matched grain a moiré pattern in taffeta.

Outside that sound cars make an amplified insistent gear a kind of gathering almost

a shudder then the dissipate a faddish motorbike compelled to speak.

Composition

The voice of a single unidentifiable bird cracking dark

an electric kettle flicked on as first step toward coffee

red plum from the fridge a small cold body in the mouth

in still-on porchlight paving stones gleam sepia

a car gone that visited the old man his swaddled news on the grass

drenched hem of the long cotton robe heavy from wet

the paper lain on the porch a cat standing on the walk

3 a.m.'s endless itemizing heart and red numbers banging change

a dream city's mute de Chirico porticoes

naked prowling against a cold window's breath

where was the old cat its death that would not surprise

Maternity

Said to me once you are a calm pond but I was pregnant then

imploded soon to be exploded

said to me once you live in a room of your own making

in desert glare on lame legs shaky pins halt gait spavined stumble

winged wobble the left behind

cool dark of still standing ruins mirrored on sand

columns with no arches temples with no roofs plinths with no busts

a life in quotes whizzy hologram

like classical statues of women meant to represent cities

nipples pinked with tinted wax

like the MGM Tara a façade no rooms inside

a desert sky at the war's end holding rain the promised green shoots

Raptors

August sun beat a rosebush into mosaic in greenglass trees
hidden bodies

the hawk whistling woke her it must want food why wouldn't it stop
the shrill of saying

in the dream a woman became her applying and reapplying
red lipstick as if the mouth not part of the face

how it kissed what it said

lipstick could make that mouth again

saying she didn't love him petting the one truly loved
like a dog or a child though what was truly or loved

someone pushing through room after room
the voice that took on muted colors of weather

a woman's laughter like a gull's velvet mezzo

the thump on the porch made her run to see what was left
a gray feathered wing
white asterisks of a spine headless but taloned

must be picked up could not be walked around

in colluding leaves feathered bodies compact as ordnance
white spatter from the trees

calls like infants crying breasts quickening

Initial Surprise at Finding the Wound

Dark triangles flattened against dusk's violet four pines at the end of a pool

a digital timer tonguing red neon over bright blue water

air slips around the skinned bark of Mexican fan palms near the Pacific
this name for water denying anger or rage

like grabbing the back of a neck like rumpling a cat's fur to lift it

words lain aside enter the house but don't find them no oiled lock slides into place

a long white hallway desk hollow as thumped watermelon or skull

ragged scraps of red felt a haystack of a mattress

bodies' vinegar fume light's furious slap
the turning tasting o quite sexual

then gone picked on scab

like large birds who fear hawks and carrion they everyday leave

The News

A German Shepherd barkblunting daylight a mewling skinny glare
solders fast leaves

a woman running a hooded guy on brightred city rentabike

circular swinging of a yardlong lanyard someone who loses her keys

a pendulum weight at the end of an arm a box lid the days hammer down

what to make of the crowsagged powerline a handclap explodes

July's startled dishwater air

the question of crossfire

come come said to the cat helplessly upended open your eyes for the clear drops

pinch the skin put in the needle how the leaves clang

did they see the news

rain bringing down charred naked hills summer fire wiping out

communities whose wealth no protection eeck eeck

from nested brown clots in leaves

September 1 Trees Already Shedding
Like Snow That Never Falls Here

Once when the cold up to my shins air gray with ice

cardboard and plywood in the car trunk for when the wheels spun

here the heat laps at the body palm fronds pierce small coins of ficus

a plane growls through a gray felt marine layer a leaf blower responds gutturally

a woman holds out a sandwich a man's clothes look slept-in

noon ices gray sage in desert yards ICED a new use that lacks luster

the man talking to the air then the nodding and sparring then snarling

a tai chi class moves minnowlike over what was Tongva land

from vined beds demotic shadows streak sidewalks

outside glass café walls the word *basura* on a bin the hand moves in and out of

night's neonsplashed fish in dull water

Hot Enough

Dark when she wakes and dark when she leaves

falling asleep still dressed and at 12 the phone

the locked-out cat mouth frozen wide in midsqueak

glass door to the balcony that makes a theatre of trees

tomorrow will be hot enough she fears it

a gaping mouth's shroud of longing to wear loosely as possible

fierce jays wait for the cat's try at crossing the yard

pyracantha drunk robins of April slam into glass

What to See from the Car

A bath of space the light that could not hide if it wanted

lavished on gray chamisa the silty earth's dry bouquets

fast driving on the mesa a risingfalling drama

the silhouettes of cows and elk roadside cautions

a café for coffee and listening a looming Alice

in the house that's always with you

topography as familiar as your body

or another's you could stand upright beneath floorbeam cobwebs

dust and funk linger nothing special about losing

the earth shifts and chasms

whips mesas out of shale and sandstone dead seas' desert residue

graduates smile down from lightpoled banners

the café's lifesized posters dead Marilyn and Audrey
a princess on a motorbike

holding tight to a stranger

Piedra

The day growing long still far from Tucson

easy to cry velvet the long purple shadows

underfoot grit of small rocks

overhead puffed and warty cloud towers

wind collects into palisades and peñas

roadside blur of sugartwined crosses

measure a land by moments of dying

the house you wore like a coat

your sleeve-succored wrist knobs

finally passing Piedra then the town Gila Bend

Desert

Look quickly at a speedometer see 90 the how can my body move at such speed

right foot slipping out then back into a sandal the high desert's graysprigged pale silk dress
you would wear though it meant death

small car in a semi's wake

keep closed the window a/c blasting knees a woman's voice froths
on the radio we must protect liberty meaning free

to infect or be infected of the world not in it
calling loudly

no one in the room

fingerraked dry hair a faucet's warm gush dark strands on white porcelain
and outside burned-to-thatch summer gardens

in acidic morning light
spider silk to blunder through

satisfied you Made Time hurtling toward a coast as the continent slid into brine

308

Curly volutes of white-iced columns called the house Victorian
a hooded ell-shaped porch a screened sleeping space
on suffocating nights kids on cots in the long yard

eyes closed to stars without fear

jam from waspy figs lemon rinds' musky syrup
bristly orbed amaranths edified a palm

December clouds flatbottomed in the hard blue the silverberried
deerlease cedar brought inside

fanned fronds pinched for the styptic thrill

her angry arrows his easy drawl the two of them
not even 30 yet their fingers' tapering
ballasts of smoke

how big were those rooms

parking the rental at 308 checking numbers for the right house
bright paint of the trim
quaint now

dark green wall papered with whitefleshed magnolias
a gas heater orange flame jumped through ceramic filigree

her on the floor the man's starched white collar
the look she gave
why don't you

o love from the radio

o cardboard thing

Years Later Where a House Might Have Been

The small child in the photo stands in front of a house weight on one leg

other knee cocked a pose suggesting knowingness but what could she know
to whom would she tell it

hackberry leaves dampmatted on gray ground they called it winter there

a chameleon leashed to a short string disappeared on her cotton dress
into floral garble

certain to have stepped on a coiled snake but it was dry land

she knew to fear rattlers the coil had not moved had there been a snake

bigeared green leaves fringed the house
sweaty earth noisy shadows

Dully Useful Chairs

A sharp gold wall in late afternoon years later

what seemed the same wall shadows fled from

summer skin sweat damp cicadas raucous in old trees

an unwashed body sour when you leaned in

leafthatched screened porch tinnitus of insect chatter

can you see where the storm came through those stripped limbs

Dog

The old cottonwood forks from the highwalled yard where the dog with a white ball in his teeth
chews tirelessly loving the squeak

when he drops it backs away I know to pick it up it has been hard for him to teach me

I do not particularly like touching a ball soaked and clotted by a slick tongue or to throw it

not having what is called an arm not even able to reach the wall

only seconds and the ball again in his mouth making that noise like car tires screeching

the cry of the damned if the damned were plastic
he flops to the grass the squeaking something alive in his teeth

Big Stone

Thunder's undertone miles overhead

in the quiet of a falling barometer I feel you

the day's cotton scarf with its blue roses night's blue dye

throat's bounty a washcloth lifts
the shower's slick wet white curtain clinging

we dried ourselves to doves' minor key whowhoing

that plain room held in my arms like swaddle each day's
big stone I lay down

the book shut tight the newsprint scrap saves the place we left off

the way ahead a penciled line between two countries

words underfoot you said pick them up I said no

like a dream the do this do that

at a river's edge sun changing cars to brass

The Body the Distance Traveled

Morning spills from the bulk of a small house its quiet hour
unyoked to must

the shaggy elms raining green benediction

the arbutus with its red fruit a baretrunked palm's spreading crest
dear to the mother of the gods

dim rooms' few mysteries of light

the leaded body and stunned mind remembering fire

like waking to a front door standing open the panicked survey what's askew no

the still gaping purse the small box with the small adornments yet

closed tight it was daylight when you came in

turning on then off the porchlight it must have been the wind
so strong anyone could have

the wanting back when you could not speak enough
from the bruised body

the ready underworld and its glimpse of anthracite

like bats the names of things cling irretrievably

time to go

your dirty clothes your smoothed skirt did you look ok your shirt

that bore no wrinkle of caring

Almost Everything Happens at the Threshold

Each stem barely holds up its head of bunched florets

crisped pink-green to bronze without metal's weight

relics of a gone city whose language undecoded

last night the rain with no warning

today trucks' weekly stopgostop lifting

curbside bins pregnant with stems limbs and cuttings

great pincers roughly upend and shake into a truck's maw

reliable these visits lacking rain's temperament

like other visits you quit expecting then had to ask

what to do where to go what will you eat

The Old Habit of Flowers
Thomas Browne, *Urne-Burial*

The glamorized exhaust-tinctured anglicized jacaranda said like *veranda* space for cocktails
a word gone from fashion

like a ruffled Cubano musician-shirt dusk-color bluewhite in clublight

above nonnative toothpick palms loved by developers that shrieking green parrots crisscross

narrow trunks rising from wilted amethyst pools of fallen tissue trumpets

ROY G BIV slideaways toward the spectrum's crepuscular possible

pixellated shimmer a familiar choreography

all around the sky continuing as small brighteyed dogs slip their leashes children chase them

the bannered sheen of almost white hair

Acknowledgments

Many thanks to the following journals and their editors in which some of these poems appear:

"Stunned Awake" and "Geometry"—to Sarah Elkamel, *Four Way Review*

"Initial Surprise at the Wound," "Hot Enough," and "Dog"—to Holaday Mason, *Furious Pure*

"308"—to Catherine Strisik, *Taos Journal of Poetry*

"The Body the Distance Traveled"—to Paul Hoover, *New American Writing*

For the generous contributions of time, spirit, and intelligence they gave to the reading and publication of these poems, I thank Gail Wronsky, Theresia de Vroom, Judy Dater, Ash Good, Leslie Ullman, Mariano Zaro, Louise Mathias, and Dell Upton.

The epigraph from Tomas Tranströmer is from *Collected Works,* "Baltics," part 3, tr. Robin Fulton.

The epigraph from Yannis Ritsos is from *Diaries of Exile,* "Dec. 3, 1948," tr. Karen Emmerich and Edmund Keeley.

KAREN KEVORKIAN is a native of San Antonio who moved to San Francisco but detoured to the east coast before returning to California and working as an editor for the Fine Arts Museums of San Francisco, teaching poetry and fiction writing workshops at UCLA, and before that at the University of Virginia. *Here in My Body It Feels Crowded* is her fourth poetry collection. Her poems are recently published in *New American Writing*, *Volt*, *Four Way Review*, *Taos Journal of Poetry*, and many other journals. She has been awarded fellowships from the Djerassi Resident Artist Program, the Ucross Foundation, the Millay Colony for the Arts, MacDowell, and the Helene Wurlitzer Foundation. In Los Angeles she was a board member for seven years of Beyond Baroque literary arts center and is a founding member of the Glass Table Collective, publisher of What Books Press.

www.ingramcontent.com/pod-product-compliance
Lightning Source LLC
Chambersburg PA
CBHW041156120626

46547CB00020B/3235